YOUR FIRST ORCHID

Stephen R. Batchelor
Photographs by Charles Marden Fitch

Series Editor James B. Watson

2001 Revised Edition

American Orchid Society
Delray Beach, Florida

American Orchid Society

Contents

Front Cover (left to right): *Sophrolaeliocattleya*
Petite's Wink, *Kagawara* Yuthayong Beauty
'TOF', AM/AOS, *Paphiopedilum* Fumi's Delight
'Suzanne', AM/AOS (inset), watering cattleya
(inset), *Phalaenopsis* Cebu (bottom right).
Back Cover (top to bottom): *Ascocenda*
Viraphandhu, *Dendrobium* Bangkok Queen

'Ho', *Brassolaeliocattleya* hybrid (*Blc.* Pokai
x *Brassolaelia* Richard Mueller).
Title Page: *Slc.* Petite's Wink and *Phal.* Cebu.
Above, left to right: *Darwinara* Charm 'Blue
Star', HCC/AOS, *Ascocenda* Bangyikhan
Gold 'Viboon', *Paphiopedilum armeniacum*,
and *Epidendrum cinnabarinum*.

Your First Orchid © 2001 American Orchid Society, 16700 AOS Lane, Delray Beach, Florida 33446-4351
(telephone 561-404-2000; fax 561-404-2100; e-mail TheAOS@aos.org; Web site orchidweb.org). Library of
Congress Catalog Card Number: 2001-132034. ISBN 0-923096-02-7. Photographs © Charles Marden Fitch.
Text © American Orchid Society. The opinions and recommendations that may appear in this publication
regarding the selection and use of specific plant-care products, including but not limited to pesticides, fungicides and herbicides, are those of the author, and not those of the American Orchid Society, which neither
adopts nor endorses such opinions and recommendations and disclaims all responsibility for them. When
selecting and using such products, readers should seek and obtain the advice of the manufacturer and of
responsible government agencies.

1 ~ Where to Grow

A FEW DAYS AGO YOU BOUGHT your first orchid at a show in the shopping mall. You were taken by the exquisite flowers and, even though you had never grown anything other than a philodendron indoors, you made the purchase. It looks great on the coffee table and no doubt will for several weeks. To prolong the show and coax it into bloom again, initiate a carefully planned maintenance program.

To begin, take the plant to the kitchen sink. Run lukewarm water into the container for about 15 seconds or until water flows through the drain holes for several seconds. Most orchids are potted in porous mixes that do not hold water the way conventional soil mixes do. This is because in nature most are epiphytic — that is, they grow on trees with their roots exposed to the air.

Above: Orchids — including the phalaenopsis here — have become popular for decorating the home, where their long-lasting flowers complement just about any decor.
Opposite: A variety of genera offer compact-growing species and hybrids that meet the need of windowsill gardeners.

Move the plant around to moisten the entire potting medium. Then, gently wash the plant to remove any dust or residue.

Check the orchid in a few days. Stick your finger an inch or so down into the medium. If it feels dry, water again. Under average conditions, you will probably need to water one or two times a week. Watering is discussed in greater detail in the next chapter.

When the flowers wither and drop, remove what is left of the flower spike with a sterile cutting edge. Make a clean cut near the base of the spike and remove any dead or yellow leaves the same way.

Your First Orchid

Be forewarned that orchids are susceptible to certain plant viruses. Since these can be transmitted by contaminated cutting edges, use a sterile cutting edge, such as a new single-edge razor blade. Once you have made the necessary cuts, either throw the used blade away or wipe it clean and resterilize in a 300 F (132 C) or warmer oven for one hour. Never use the same cutting edge for more than one plant (unless it has been sterilized between uses).

Your Orchid's Basic Needs

Now you need to find a place to grow your orchid. But before you do, consider the plant's requirements. In addition to water, your orchid must have:

- Bright Light — Direct sunlight at least two hours a day or fluorescent light (preferably from wide-spectrum tubes) at least 14 hours a day for most types of orchids.
- Moderate Temperatures — Conditions in which you are comfortable, with ideally a 15-degree F (10-degree C) drop at night.

- Moist, Fresh Air — Like a gentle summer breeze off a lake.

Light Requirements How much light your orchid will need depends on what kind it is. When orchidists talk in general terms, they usually mention orchids by genus. Scientists identify living things with two names: first the genus name and then the specific epithet. Together they form the species name. Any number of related species and/or hybrids comprise the genus.

Look at the plant's label. The first name should be the genus name. Locate that name in the chart on page 9 to find your orchid's light needs, along with an idea of where you could grow it.

Temperature Requirements Cultivated orchids are classified as cool growing, intermediate or warm growing. These groups reflect their relative tolerance for temperature extremes, a tolerance determined by the origins of the orchid's parentage. Species found in the lower elevations of the tropics are considered warmer growing, while species found only at higher elevations are generally cooler growing.

Opposite: The vast majority of orchids are epiphytes, or air plants, that typically grow on the trunks and limbs of trees. Knowing how orchids grow in nature, such as these laelias and epidendrums in El Salvador, often makes it easier to understand and meet their cultural needs. *Above:* Plenty of light induces orchids growing on a windowsill to flower.

Although your orchid's ancestors probably came from the tropics, this does not mean you have to keep it warm to hot at all times. Most orchids would not grow well under a constant high temperature. Ideally, day temperatures should be 70 to 80 F (21 to 27 C), with night temperatures about 15 F (10 C) cooler, around 50 to 65 F (10 to 18 C).

Indoor locations do not always experience this broad a daily range in temperatures. But just because the thermostat is kept at one setting does not mean your orchid will be exposed to a constant temperature. Temperature varies tremendously from place to place. Your orchid in a sunny window may experience a far greater variation in temperature than that thermostat mounted on the interior wall. If you want a more accurate idea of what temperatures

Getting Started

HERE'S a shopping list of what you'll need to begin. The first two items can be found at a hardware store and most general-purpose stores:

Single-edge razor blades (A box of five or so.)

Thermometer (A cheap one will do, but if your pocketbook allows, invest in the more expensive maximum-minimum thermometers. One look each day and you'll know more about the temperatures your orchid is experiencing.)

The following four items are found at many garden centers (but not all — call ahead):

Plant hangers (Preferably those with clamps that firmly grasp the rim of the pot.)

Orchid potting mix (Preferably containing a mixture of organic and inorganic components, such as bark, perlite and charcoal.)

Orchid fertilizer (Choose a water-soluble formula; 30-10-10 if your orchid is in bark, 20-20-20 if it is not.)

Pots (Clay or plastic, 6-, 8- and 10-inch diameter containers. Orchid pots with slits are optional.)

your orchid is experiencing, place a thermometer as near to the plant as possible (but out of direct sunlight). Check it throughout a typical day and night. Or, buy a maximum-minimum thermometer — it will give you the temperature extremes of any one day at a glance.

For short periods of time (hours, not days), orchids can withstand temperatures as low as the low 40s F (5 to 7 C) and as high as more than 90 F (32 C) without being hurt. Certainly these conditions occur frequently outdoors. If you are growing your orchid outside, bring it in on those nights when temperatures are forecast to dip below 50 F (10 C). If the daytime temperatures are expected to exceed 90 F (32 C), move your plant to a shadier location for the duration of the heat wave, and water adequately.

See the chart on page 10 for the temperature classifications of the more popular genera.

Humidity and Air Movement Orchids prefer moist fresh air. This is difficult to achieve indoors, where air conditioning and heating dry the atmosphere. If you have

Above: During the summer, many orchids can be placed outside on a shaded patio. In South Florida, Hawaii and other tropical regions, orchids can be raised outdoors year round.

your orchid indoors, you might want to place it on a tray of gravel in which a constant level of water is maintained just below the top of the rocks. This water will evaporate around your plant, raising the humidity. Operating a humidifier when the heat is on may also be beneficial. Unless you live in an arid climate, adequate humidity should not be a problem if you decide to grow your orchids outdoors during warm weather.

Finding the Right Spot
Many places in and around the home and office can fulfill the needs outlined above. Consider these locations:
- A sunny window
- Under fluorescent lights
- Outdoors

A Sunny Window If you have a large window in your home that receives direct sunlight for at least a couple of hours each

Light Requirements by Genus

Genus	Light Requirements*	Growing Areas (1 - Ideal, 2 - Suitable, 3 - Adequate)
Cattleya Alliance (*Brassavola, Cattleya, Epidendrum, Laelia, Sophronitis* and hybrids)	Medium to high	1. Outdoors 2. In a sunny window 3. Under fluorescent lights
Cymbidium	Medium to high	1. Outdoors 2. In a sunny window
Dendrobium	Medium to high	1. Outdoors 2. In a sunny window
Masdevallia	Low to medium	1. Under fluorescent lights 2. In a window with shading 3. Outdoors with shading
Miltonia	Medium	1. Outdoors 2. In a moderately sunny window 3. Under fluorescent lights
Odontoglossum	Medium	1. Outdoors 2. In a moderately sunny window 3. Under fluorescent lights
Oncidium	Medium to high	1. Outdoors 2. In a sunny window 3. Under fluorescent lights
Paphiopedilum	Low to medium	1. Under fluorescent lights 2. In a window with shading or outdoors with shading
Phalaenopsis	Low to medium	1. Under fluorescent lights 2. In a window with shading or outdoors with shading
Vanda Alliance (*Aerides, Ascocentrum, Vanda* and hybrids)	Medium to high	1. Outdoors 2. In a very sunny window

*Low light — 1,000-2,000 foot-candles (see definition below), two hours of filtered sunlight per day, 14 hours of fluorescent light within 8 inches (20 cm) of the tubes.

Medium light — 2,000-3,000 foot-candles, four hours of sunlight per day, 16 hours of fluorescent light within 6 inches (15 cm) of the tubes.

High light — 3,000-4,000 foot-candles, six hours of sunlight per day, within 3 inches (7.5 cm) of tubes, near the center of the fixture.

Foot-candles is a standard measure of light for plants and can be determined with a light meter. Most growers, however, go by the average hours of sunlight or fluorescent light per day.

day, this would be an appropriate place to start growing your orchid. To take advantage of the light, set the plant close to the windowpane. Place the pot on the windowsill if the ledge is wide enough to hold the container. If the sill is too narrow, you can either place a table or other surface near the window and set the plant on that, or hang the orchid from the blinds or curtain rod.

Make sure the orchid is not touching the glass. In the winter in a cold climate, leaves touching the windowpane may freeze.

If the window receives more than four hours of unbroken sunlight around midday, shade your orchid to keep the excess light from burning (damaging) the leaves. Hang blinds, which when partially open create alternating bars of light and shade, or, sheer curtains. Draping cheesecloth between the window and plant is an alternative.

Should you live where there are no sunny windows, consider where you work. Many offices have windows that are terrific for raising orchids.

Orchids, like other plants, grow toward light. If you decide to raise your plant in a window, every week or two turn the plant 180 degrees. Should you not do this, in time your orchid will be lopsided. (While the plant is in bud, however, do not rotate it. If you do, the stems will twist and the flowers will not display themselves properly.)

Under Fluorescent Lights Even if you work in a windowless office, you may be able to grow your orchid there. Interior offices brightly lit with fluorescent lights can support a jungle growth of plants. But before you try growing your orchids under such artificial lighting, make certain:

- There are four-tube fixtures, as is the case in most offices. Replace office fluorescent tubes with those especially designed for plants. These can be purchased at most garden centers and hardware stores.
- You can place the plant within 6 inches (15 cm) of the lights, and near the center of the fixture if at all possible. In many large offices, partitions do not reach the ceiling. The tops of these dividers, if wide enough, are a convenient way to place plants near lighting.
- The lights are left on after work hours. To flower most orchids, fluorescent lights have to be on at least 14 hours a day. If this cannot be done at your office, look elsewhere to grow your orchid — or consider buying a light cart.

Temperature and Orchids

Temperature Classification	Recommended Temperature Range	Genera*
Cool growing	Minimum Night: 50 F (10 C) Maximum Day: 80 F (27 C)	*Cymbidium, Masdevallia, Miltonia, Odontoglossum, Oncidium, Paphiopedilum* (green leaves), *Sophronitis*
Intermediate	Minimum Night: 55 F (13 C) Maximum Day: 85 F (30 C)	*Brassavola, Cattleya, Dendrobium, Epidendrum, Laelia, Paphiopedilum* (mottled leaves)
Warm growing	Minimum Night: 60 F (15 C) Maximum Day: 90 F (32 C)	*Phalaenopsis, Vanda*

*These classifications are based on the genus as a whole. However, a range of temperature tolerance can be found within each genus.

The Orchid Family

THE Orchidaceae is one of the largest families of flowering plants in the plant kingdom. There are 25,000 named species (and possibly as many as 35,000 species) in nature. Distributed worldwide, the majority come from the Old World and New World Tropics, where they are generally epiphytes — plants growing on other plants that are called hosts (usually trees). It is these orchids that were first brought into cultivation in England in the middle of the 19th century. Other orchids are lithophytes (growing on rocks) and many in temperate regions are terrestrials (in the ground).

Available at some garden centers, or through orchid suppliers, light carts provide the perfect environment in which to grow orchids requiring less illumination. Buy a timer, so you can reliably set the hours the lights are on each day.

Outdoors Whether you live in an apartment or a house, consider the possibility of placing your orchid outdoors during the warmer months.

Many apartments have balconies or patios. If yours is sunny part of the day, it might be appropriate for your orchid. But

Above: Maximum-minimum thermometers are ideal for measuring temperatures in microclimates.
Below: Air conditioning and heating make it difficult to provide the moist fresh air orchids prefer. One solution is a portable humidifier, ideal for a collection of orchids and other houseplants.

Above: Orchid enthusiasts often develop elaborate setups to meet the needs of their expanding hobby. Here, an apartment dweller installed shelves illuminated with broad-spectrum fluorescent tubes. A timer turns the lights on and off automatically.

Above: Trays filled with gravel and water increase humidity around orchids. Adjust the water level so it comes to just below the surface of the gravel.

Climate

I. Temperate

    A. New England, the Midwest, the Northwest

    B. The South

        1. Interior (including Central Texas)

        2. Gulf Coast (including East Texas), North and Central Florida

II. Subtropical (South Florida)

III. Tropical (Hawaii)

IV. Arctic/Subarctic (Alaska)

V. Arid (Southwest, Interior California)

VI. Mediterranean/Maritime (West Coast)

north-facing recessed patios and balconies rarely receive adequate light to coax an orchid to flower. Where unrelenting sunlight strikes, take special precautions. Try hanging the orchid beneath the eaves, where it will receive shading from the midday sun. If you have other plants in this location, use them to shade your orchid, at least at first. Balconies facing the ocean are unsuitable; salt spray harms orchids.

Beyond your dwelling lie other suitable environments. Consider hanging your orchid from a tree, a clothesline, an old swing set or a fence, or place it on a patio. These could all be satisfactory growing spots for your orchid, so long as you can provide some shading from the midday sun and protection from temperatures below 50 F (10 C) and above 90 F (32 C).

See the chart below — Where to Grow Based on Where You Live — for where to grow your orchid, based on your location and the time of year.

Orchid Societies

FOR specific growing advice for your area, talk to other orchid growers in your region. See how they grow orchids to get yourself off to a good start. Some may grow orchids in a greenhouse, while others cultivate their collection in the home. Wherever they grow, they should be able to offer practical advice that will help you to select species and hybrids with which to begin, and help you create your own orchid-growing environment.

The American Orchid Society has more than 500 Affiliated Societies worldwide. They are listed in the *AOS Orchid Source Directory,* which is updated every two years and sent to all Society members. Consult it to locate the Affiliated Society nearest you or inquire at AOS Headquarters to see if a new group has been established close to where you live.

Joining a local society has benefits: regular meetings, a newsletter, annual show and sale, and becoming friends with others who enjoy cultivating orchids.

Where to Grow Based on Where You Live

Winter	Spring	Summer	Autumn
indoors	indoors until after frost	outdoors	outdoors until frost
indoors	outdoors/protect as needed	outdoors	outdoors/protect as needed
outdoors/protect as needed	outdoors	outdoors	outdoors/protect as needed
outdoors/protect as needed	outdoors	outdoors	outdoors
outdoors	outdoors	outdoors	outdoors
indoors	indoors	indoors	indoors
indoors	indoors	indoors	indoors
outdoors/protect as needed	outdoors/protect as needed	outdoors	outdoors/protect as needed

2 ~ Watering and Fertilizing

Above: When watering orchids in a sink, place the container on a plastic mesh tray to keep the potting mix from washing into the drain. A sprinkler attached to a flexible hose makes it easy to direct water onto the medium.

Opposite: One way to determine if an orchid needs watering is to push your finger down into the top 1 inch of the medium. Water if it is dry. An alternative is to insert a sharpened pencil to the same depth. If the pencil tip is moist, wait awhile before watering.

YOU'VE FOUND A SUITABLE PLACE to grow your orchid. Proper watering and fertilizing is necessary to induce it to flower again.

Remember, because most orchids in cultivation are epiphytes (grow on trees in nature), they are potted in a very porous (open) medium. This has two immediate consequences:

- The orchid medium will not hold water. Shortly after you pour water into the pot, it will drain out the bottom. Water where the plant can drain without causing harm.
- The mix will appear to dry quickly. Resist the temptation to water just because the surface of the potting medium looks dry. It is easy for beginners to overwater their orchids — so beware.

How Often to Water

On the average, most growers water their orchids once or twice a week. This is enough for most potted orchids growing in a sunny window. But if you have your plant outdoors, and it is sunny, warm and dry, you might need to water every other day. On the other hand, if it has been cloudy and cool, once a week could be enough.

Your orchid's water needs depend on a number of variables. Light, temperature, humidity, air movement, potting medium, type of pot and pot size all affect the amount of water your orchid requires. The best orchid growers adjust their watering schedules to the conditions their plants are experiencing. The table on page 17 should help you decide whether you should water more often, or less.

The best way, though, to decide whether to water is to check the potting medium. This is where most of the roots are — and it is the roots, after all, that absorb water. Remember, the surface of the medium will dry quickly. What you need to determine is whether the medium is dry below the surface (where the roots are located). There are two ways to do this:

- Stick your finger or the sharp end of a pencil down into the potting medium 1 inch or more. If the medium feels wet or the pencil is moist, delay watering a few days and check again. Water when the medium feels moist, but not entirely dry.
- Water by weight. Lift your orchid an hour or so after you next water. Make a mental note of how much it weighs

— or actually weigh it on a scale. Lift or weigh it again in a few days, and, when it feels significantly lighter, water. If you do this enough, you will develop a sense by weight of when the plant is dry.

Whenever you water, be sure to:

- Use lukewarm water. (Cold water could shock your orchid.)
- Wet all sections of the plant's container.
- Apply enough water to flush the potting medium thoroughly. (This also helps minimize salt build-up, which can damage roots.)

Fertilizing

In nature most orchids grow off the ground, usually in trees, where the nutrients that reach them in water runoff are dilute. It only follows, then, that your orchid will not need copious amounts of fertilizer. The type of fertilizer you use, though, is important.

An Exception

THE recommendations given here for fertilizing your orchid are generalized. There are exceptions, of course.

Cycnoches (SIK-no-kees) and *Catasetum* (kat-a-SEE-tum), orchids from Central and South America, have an annual growth cycle. In the spring and summer they grow rapidly. In the autumn and winter they do not grow, but undergo a period of rest.

Hobbyists have discovered that during active growth these orchids greatly benefit from large amounts of fertilizer. Where one-quarter teaspoon of fertilizer is recommended, they use one tablespoon. Because these plants are growing so fast they are able to make use of all of these nutrients. Conversely, when cycnoches and catasetums enter their annual rest period (winter), growers withhold all, or nearly all, fertilizer and water sparingly.

Successful growers usually modify their watering and fertilizing practices to meet their orchids' changing needs.

Orchid fertilizers are sold at most garden centers. Water-soluble orchid fertilizers are designed to be diluted with water and then applied to the plant. They are the safest way to fertilize your orchid. Never apply a dry fertilizer, such as lawn fertilizer, on your orchid. It will destroy the roots.

Orchid fertilizers come in varying formulas. A fertilizer formula is made up of three numbers separated by dashes. The first number indicates the percentage of nitrogen (promotes vegetative growth), the second the percentage of phosphorus (promotes bud development and flowering) and the third the percentage of potassium (strengthens roots).

These three elements are essential for plant growth, and are needed in significant quantities. Other nutrients are required by orchids, but in small amounts. Water and potting media usually have enough of these minor nutrients to satisfy most orchids.

Three formula ratios of orchid fertilizers are commonly sold:

- 3-1-1. Examples are 30-10-10 and 15-5-5. This ratio is recommended for orchids potted in bark mixes. The extra nitrogen satisfies the orchid's needs and those of the microorganisms that cause the bark to decompose. If your orchid appears to be potted in medium composed predominantly of bark chunks, use a fertilizer with this ratio of elements.
- 1-1-1. Examples are 20-20-20 and 23-19-17. These even-formula fertilizers meet the needs of orchids rooted in potting media that do not contain bark, and for mounted orchids.
- 1-3-2. An example is 10-30-20. Often called blossom boosters, fertilizers with this formula ratio provide more phosphorus, which promotes flowering (and rooting). They are generally applied just prior to bud formation.

How Much Fertilizer to Use

The orchid fertilizer container will include information on how much to use.

Most recommend mixing one-quarter to one-half teaspoon of the fertilizer in a gallon of water. Often a measuring spoon is supplied in the container. If you have only one or two orchids, you may need to mix only one-half gallon of fertilizer solution. Reduce the amount of fertilizer you use by half the recommendation.

As a beginning guideline, apply this fertilizer solution to your orchid in place of a watering once a week when the plant is growing and once every other week when it is not. Doing so will supply the plant with a steady diet of nutrients.

When you get the hang of it, you may want to experiment with different fertilizers and frequencies. The key, as with all cultural practices, is to watch the plant closely to see how it responds.

How to Fertilize

Follow this procedure to fertilize your orchid:

- If the mix is exceptionally dry, water it first (this eliminates any chance of the fertilizer burning the roots).
- Using a measuring spoon, place the recommended amount of fertilizer in a pitcher or other container and fill with lukewarm water. The fertilizer should dissolve quickly. (Many fertilizers contain a dye that causes the water to turn blue or some other color.)

Above: Laeliocattleya Mary Ellen Carter 'Dixie Hummingbird' is among the many orchids that benefit from drying slightly between waterings.

- Pour the diluted fertilizer through your orchid's potting mix as if you were watering. If you have some of the solution left over, save it for the next time you plan to fertilize. Stir it before using it again.

Do not overfertilize your orchid. Hobbyists are inclined to think the more the better, but this is not true.

Adjusting How Often You Water

Water MORE often when:	Water LESS often when:
there's more light	there's less light
the temperatures are higher	the temperatures are lower
the humidity is lower	the humidity is higher
there's more air movement	there's less air movement
the plant has thin leaves and growths	the plant has thick leaves and growths
the plant is mounted on a slab or is growing in a basket	the plant is in a pot
the pot is small	the pot is large
the pot is clay (porous)	the pot is plastic (nonporous)

3 ~ What Kind Is It?

Above: Variation within a species inspires many orchidists to tag clones with cultivar names. Shown here are two forms of *Brassavola nodosa*, one from Costa Rica (*left*) and the other from Cozumel, Mexico (*right*).

NOW THAT YOU ARE PROVIDING the essentials to your orchid, you can take the time to figure out what kind you have. With this information you can then better determine your plant's needs.

Several resources exist for identifying orchids — nurseries, Affiliated Societies, other orchid hobbyists and myriad reference books — so you can place a name on your plant. With a little sleuthing, it is often possible to identify your first orchid so you can then learn about its origins and potential.

Identifying Your Orchid

To be properly identified, an orchid must have at least two elements to its name. They should appear in the following order:
- The genus name.
- The specific or hybrid epithet.

Together these elements compose the species or hybrid name. Sometimes, but not always, a third element, the cultivar name, is included.

By way of illustration, take a look at the label below:

> Slc. Jewel Box 'Scheherazade',
> AM/AOS
> (Anzac x Cattleya aurantiaca)

- *Slc.* is the standard abbreviation for the genus name *Sophrolaeliocattleya,* a combination of the genera (plural for genus, pronounced JEN-e-ra) *Sophronitis, Laelia* and *Cattleya.* The first letter of the genus name is always capitalized. The genus is either italicized (as here) or underlined (as above).
- Jewel Box is the hybrid, or grex, name for an artificial cross (given above in parentheses). Hybrid names are capitalized but not italicized or underlined. In contrast, the names of species (orchids made by nature) are not capitalized, but they are italicized or underlined.

- 'Scheherazade' is the cultivar name, which is the name assigned to a single genetic entity of a species or hybrid. In this case the cultivar received an Award of Merit from the American Orchid Society. A standard abbreviation, AM/AOS, is used to designate this award and should be included in any reference to the plant. Note that the cultivar name is set off in single quotation marks.

The Source on Orchid Hybrid Names

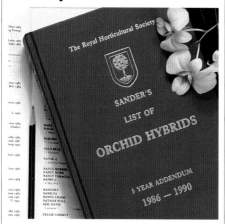

FOR an orchid hybrid to be officially named, it must be registered with the Royal Horticultural Society (RHS) of England. The RHS publishes new orchid hybrid names in each bimonthly issue of *The Orchid Review,* and this list is reprinted in various orchid periodicals around the world. This data is summarized in *Sander's List of Orchid Hybrids,* which is updated every three to five years with a new addendum. This book contains the names of all orchid hybrids registered during the previous three to five years. A search engine for orchid hybrid names on the RHS Web site is easily reached from a link on orchidweb.org.

If your orchid is identified by cross only, or you do not know what its genus abbreviation stands for, consult *Sander's.* Your local orchid society should have a copy of at least one of the addenda.

When shopping for orchids, the cultivar name is important. If you buy a plant labeled *Slc.* Jewel Box 'Scheherazade' (with or without its award included), you should be getting a plant identical to the one above, with the same flowers. However, if you buy a plant labeled *Slc.* Jewel Box 'Brand X', you're getting a different cultivar, with no guarantee its flowers will look at all like those of 'Scheherazade'.

The same would be true if you bought a plant labeled just *Slc.* Jewel Box. The absence of a cultivar name indicates that the plant has not been named yet. Name or no name, though, it is still a genetically distinct entity, with its own unique characteristics. (Possibly the owner forgot to include the cultivar name and it is really 'Scheherazade' — but you do not know and it is not worth taking the chance.)

Now check your orchid's tag. Use the following guidelines to determine whether the plant is a species or hybrid:

- If there is one word following the genus name or abbreviation, and it's not capitalized, but italicized or underlined, then you have a species. Example: *Cattleya aurantiaca.*
- If there is one word or more following the genus name, and it or they are capitalized and not italicized or underlined, then you have a hybrid. Example: *Slc.* Anzac.

Which genus your orchid belongs to, and whether it is a species or hybrid, become significant when you seek more information about its cultural needs. Most growing information pertaining to orchids is listed under the genus name, and occasionally by species. Cultural needs of hybrids, especially intergeneric hybrids (involving more than one genus), are trickier to describe, because of the ill-defined influence in breeding of one genus over another.

Monopodial Versus Sympodial

Another important way orchids are categorized is by growth habit. Orchids are either monopodial or sympodial.

Monopodial Orchids Monopodial (mon-o-POH-dee-al) orchids grow upward from a terminal growing point. This means that, once mature, these orchids will grow taller, but not much wider.

Phalaenopsis is a good example of a genus of a monopodial orchid — and an excellent choice for beginners. A phalaenopsis has an upright stem. New leaves emerge every so often from the top of this stem. Roots initiate and grow below the leaves. Phalaenopsis roots often grow right out of the pot into the open air (which is how they grow in nature). Flower spikes arise from the lower part of the stem.

Phalaenopsis are slow growers once mature, and the bottom of the stem dies off with age, so you rarely see a tall one. Because they grow vertically, not horizontally, adult phalaenopsis and other monopodial orchids do not outgrow their pots the way sympodial orchids do.

Other monopodial genera commonly grown include *Vanda* and *Angraecum* and their related genera.

Above left: Aranda Christine, at Mandai Gardens, in Singapore, exhibits the monopodial growth habit, which is also seen in vandas and phalaenopsis.
Above: Brassavola nodosa is a sympodial orchid.

Sympodial Orchids The stem of a sympodial (sim-POH-di-al) orchid grows horizontally, and is called a rhizome (RHI-zohm). From the rhizome, roots grow down and lateral shoots grow up. These shoots grow to a certain height, and stop. As a result, a sympodial orchid can get only so tall, while it can grow horizontally without limit.

Cattleya — another excellent choice for beginners — exhibits the typical sympodial growth habit. A cattleya's rhizome is located on the surface of the potting medium. The shoots growing more or less vertically from the rhizome form thickened stems called pseudobulbs (SOO-doh-bulbs). One or more leaves are at the top of each pseudobulb.

New growth in sympodial orchids usually begins at the base of the leading pseudobulb(s) from what is called an "eye"

A Cattleya by Many Names

USUALLY when orchidists speak of cattleyas they are not speaking strictly of the genus *Cattleya*. In fact, they may not be talking about *Cattleya* species or hybrids at all, but related genera.

The genus *Cattleya* is allied with several closely related genera, which collectively are known as the *Cattleya* Alliance. Members of the *Cattleya* Alliance have been interbred for decades, creating intergeneric hybrids. The genus name of these hybrids may or may not reflect its component genera. For example, it is evident that a *Sophrolaeliocattleya* hybrid is *Cattleya*-like, but the affinities of an orchid with the genus name *Potinara* are less clear.

Here is a short list of the more popular hybrid genera of the *Cattleya* Alliance. All hybrids bearing these genus names would be considered cattleyas. For a complete listing, see the front of an addendum of *Sander's List of Orchid Hybrids*.

Hybrid Genus	Abbreviation	Component Genera
Arizara	*Ariz.*	*Cattleya* x *Domingoa* x *Epidendrum*
Brassolaeliocattleya	*Blc.*	*Brassavola* x *Cattleya* x *Laelia*
Cattleytonia	*Ctna.*	*Broughtonia* x *Cattleya*
Epicattleya	*Epc.*	*Cattleya* x *Epidendrum*
Epilaeliocattleya	*Eplc.*	*Cattleya* x *Epidendrum* x *Laelia*
Kirchara	*Kir.*	*Cattleya* x *Epidendrum* x *Laelia* x *Sophronitis*
Laeliocatonia	*Lctna.*	*Broughtonia* x *Cattleya* x *Laelia*
Laeliocattleya	*Lc.*	*Cattleya* x *Laelia*
Otaara	*Otr.*	*Brassavola* x *Broughtonia* x *Cattleya* x *Laelia*
Potinara	*Pot.*	*Brassavola* x *Cattleya* x *Laelia* x *Sophronitis*
Schombocattleya	*Smbc.*	*Cattleya* x *Schomburgkia*
Sophrocattleya	*Sc.*	*Cattleya* x *Sophronitis*
Sophrolaelia	*Sl.*	*Laelia* x *Sophronitis*
Sophrolaeliocattleya	*Slc.*	*Cattleya* x *Laelia* x *Sophronitis*
Vaughnara	*Vnra.*	*Brassavola* x *Cattleya* x *Epidendrum*
Westara	*Wsta.*	*Cattleya* x *Brassavola* x *Broughtonia* x *Laelia* x *Schomburgkia*
Yamadara	*Yam.*	*Brassavola* x *Cattleya* x *Epidendrum* x *Laelia*

(a patch of cells capable of rapid division). With most healthy and mature cattleyas, the sequence of growth is this: Pseudobulb → Leaf or leaves → Flower sheath → Flowers.

The flower sheath emerges from the top of the pseudobulb at the base of the leaf. Flower buds develop within the sheath, which is typically shaped much like the sheath of a knife. With some cattleyas, the flowers develop shortly after the sheath appears, while with others they form months later after the sheath has dried and turned brown.

Immature (seedling or mericlone) cattleyas produce what are called "blind" growths — ones without sheaths, or flow-ers. Be patient; the plant should mature within a year or two and begin to flower regularly. If, on the other hand, you have a cattleya that has flowered before (you can tell by looking at the top of the old pseudobulbs for what is left of old flower stalks), and a new growth does not produce a sheath, then your plant is unhealthy.

With each new growth, the rhizome lengthens, so that usually within a couple of years a cattleya or other sympodial orchid will grow over the edge of its pot and will need to be repotted.

Other commonly grown sympodial orchids include *Cymbidium*, *Dendrobium*, *Miltonia*, *Odontoglossum*, *Oncidium* and *Paphiopedilum*.

Similar forms and coloration do not necessarily mean several plants are in the same genus. Consider this trio of members of the *Cattleya* Alliance.

Above left: Laeliocattleya Spring Velvet (Cositas Spring x Susan Holguin).

Above: Cattleytonia Rosy Jewel 'Ewa' (*Cattleya bowringiana* x *Broughtonia sanguinea*) is a bigeneric cross.

Left: The species *Cattleya labiata* var. *autumnalis* is native to Brazil.

Above: Shown here are two clones of *Cattleya* Helene Garcia, which are seedlings from one capsule. Both flowers are similar in overall shape. However, the lip of the flower on the right is closed and has a darker shade of yellow in the throat with a pink margin apically, while the flower on the left has an open lip and is lighter yellow in the throat with only a hint of color on the edge.

4 ~ Repotting Orchids

KEEPING YOUR ORCHID IN FRESH potting material is essential to its health. Sometimes, repotting will be necessary.

Potting Media

The majority of orchids in cultivation are epiphytes (EP-i-fites), meaning that in nature they grow on other plants (mostly trees). Consequently orchid roots are most at home when exposed to the air.

In cultivation, however, it is more convenient to grow orchids in containers. Various materials, called potting media, are used to fill those containers.

For a potting medium to be suitable for epiphytic orchids, it must be highly porous (have many air pockets even when packed into a container); be available, inexpensive and easy to use; and retain its porous quality for at least two years.

Many materials fit these criteria and are currently employed. They may be or-

ganic, such as bark chunks, or inorganic, such as gravel. The most versatile media are mixes of both organic and inorganic components. These media are best for beginners.

What to Buy

Many, but not all garden centers carry orchid potting media, so call ahead. Be sure to buy a bag clearly identified as suitable for orchids. If available, choose one with a mixture of ingredients, such as bark, charcoal and perlite. If you cannot find such a mix, pure (100 percent) bark or tree fern will do. Common components of orchid media are compared on page 26.

Some potting materials, such as bark and tree fern, are sold by grades (the relative size of the average piece). Three grades are commonly available: fine, medium and coarse.

Opposite: Before potting orchids, soak the medium in water overnight so it will absorb, not repel, water. Here, water is poured over New Zealand sphagnum moss, which is popular for potting phalaenopsis and other orchids.
Above: Moisten osmunda before use. To improve drainage, place clay pot shards (foreground) in the bottom of the container.
Right: A new growth and roots on a sophrolaeliocattleya indicate it is time to repot.

Medium grades are suitable for most orchids; fine grades are better for seedlings and small orchids; and coarse grades are preferable for orchids in large pots (greater than 8 inches in diameter) and certain types of orchids, such as vandas.

Never use bagged mulches intended for use around the yard for your orchid. They consist of materials not suitable for orchids.

When to Repot

Most orchid growers usually repot every other year during spring or summer.

After two years, organic potting mixes decompose. The resulting material, which resembles peat moss, is highly absorbent and prevents enough air from reaching the roots. Repot before this happens or the roots may die.

Like other plants, orchids tend to grow during warmer weather and will re-establish more quickly when repotted at this time. Ideally, you want to repot after flowering, when new roots are just forming and are less than $1/2$ inch long.

But what about your first orchid? When was it last repotted? You do not know. Wait until warm weather and repot when:

- New roots are just beginning to grow.
- The plant has outgrown its container, or the medium shows signs of deterioration.

Signs that a potting medium should be replaced include:

- A lowering of the potting medium level well below the rim of the pot.
- A delay in its drying out.
- The appearance of white crust around the inside rim of the pot (meaning salts from the water and fertilizer have accumulated).
- Being able to stick your finger down into the medium without much resistance.

Repotting Materials

Here is a short list of the supplies you will need:

- Potting media
- A one-gallon bucket
- A new pot (if your plant has outgrown its old pot)
- Stakes and rhizome clips
- Sterile single-edge razor blades or other sterile cutting implement
- Old newspaper
- Plant labels (available at garden centers) and a soft-lead (No. 1) pencil
- A toothbrush

Common Components of Orchid Media

Component	Appearance	Comments
Fir bark	Chunks of reddish brown bark in various grades (fine, medium and coarse)	Major component of many commercial mixes
Tree fern	Thin black sticks of varying lengths or grades	Often used by itself or with a small percentage of perlite
Osmunda	Large chunks of fibrous dark-brown-to-black fern root	Once popular, now rarely seen. Difficult to use properly. Not generally recommended for beginners
Charcoal (not briquettes)	Black and dusty chunks in various grades	Minor component of many mixes
Perlite	Little white balls of varying grades	Synthetic, does not decompose. Holds water and helps maintain aeration in organic mixes
Gravel, lava rock, etc.	Naturally occurring or synthetic materials of varying grades	Inorganic, do not decompose. Not commonly used by beginners

Preparation for Repotting

The night before you plan to repot, place enough potting medium in the bucket to repot the plant. Use a pot the same size to measure, or, if you are moving the plant into a larger pot, use it. Cover with water and allow to soak overnight. This will prime the medium for use; otherwise, it could resist absorbing water and your orchid could desiccate. You may want to pour off this water when you are ready to repot the next day — but not down a drain, which it could clog.

Check also to see that your orchid's current medium is moist. This will make it easier to remove the next day. If it is on the dry side, water now. Last, lay out the newspaper and put all the things you need on it. Remove a sheet of newspaper each time you repot a plant.

As mentioned in the previous chapter, whether you have a monopodial or sympodial orchid will determine how you repot. First, review that information to determine the growth habit of your orchid. Then follow the appropriate directions below for monopodial and sympodial orchids.

Repotting Monopodial Orchids

Phalaenopsis is the most common genus of monopodial orchids in cultivation so it will be the subject of this discussion.

Remember that mature monopodial orchids generally do not outgrow their pots, so this should not be a criterion for repotting. *Phalaenopsis*, and related hybrid genera (*Doritaenopsis*, for example), prefer to be repotted at least once every other year. Some growers repot annually with good results.

Step 1. Take the plant out of the pot Remove any hanger from the pot. Place the stem between your index and middle finger of one hand and your other hand on the bottom of the container. Now turn the pot upside down and shake while pulling down. Most phalaenopsis will dislodge in this manner.

Above: When selecting a new container, choose one that is only 1 or 2 inches larger than the present vessel. The cattleya shown here has been over-potted and the extra medium around the roots may hold excessive moisture that could cause the roots' health to suffer.

Step 2. Clean the plant of all potting mix Using a new razor blade or other sterile cutting edge, remove any dead roots that remain attached to the base of the stem. Dead roots appear dark brown and their soft outer coating often slips off. Living roots are whiter, harder and intact. Cut any broken roots cleanly behind the break. Remove any dead leaves and old inflorescences.

Step 3. Clean the old pot With an old toothbrush and water, scrape and scrub all surfaces of the pot. Be sure to remove any salt residues, which appear as white deposits particularly along the inside rim of the pot. If the pot has only one drainage hole, you might add a 1-inch-deep layer of inorganic material, such as styrofoam packing chips, gravel or crock (pieces of clay pots). This is optional if the pot has four or more drainage holes around its base and the pot itself is less than 8 inches in diameter.

Step 4. Place the plant into the pot Make

Paphiopedilums are sympodial orchids that require dividing periodically. Step 1. The red tag in this specimen indicates where an old center growth died. This offers a natural dividing point.

Step 2. Remove the plant from the container and shake the medium off of the roots. Cut off dead roots and divide the plant into pieces.

sure that most if not all of the roots are inside. If the majority of the roots do not fit comfortably within the pot, use a larger container. With one hand, hold the plant around the base of the stem so that it is centered in the pot and its lowermost leaves are level with the top of the rim. With the other hand, add the potting mix. Firmly pack the mix down until the plant is fairly stable.

Step 5. Water the plant While you are so doing, wash off any potting medium on the leaves. See below for care after repotting.

Step 6. Transfer the label If the old label is broken or hard to read, make a new one. Also, write the month and the year on the back of the label. This way, when you next consider repotting you will know when you last did.

Repotting Sympodial Orchids

Cattleya is the most common genus of sympodial orchids in cultivation so it will be the subject of this discussion.

Sympodial orchids, such as cattleyas, need repotting when the rhizome grows

Step 3. Repot each division into its own container. Set the division in place, then ladle the medium around the roots and firm.

Step 4. After potting each division, insert a label with the plant's name into each container. Water each plant and place in a lightly shaded area before returning the plant to the growing area.

over the edge of the pot. Even if your plant has not done this, you should still repot if it has been more than two years (the potting medium will have begun to decompose).

Step 1. Remove the plant from its pot
Cattleyas, particularly if they have been in the pot for some time, can be far more of a challenge to extricate from their pots than phalaenopsis. Soak the roots to allow them to become pliable and easier to remove. Try gently bending the plant from side to side. Most of the roots adhere to the inside surface of the pot and this will help separate

Getting a Handle on Razor Blades

CUTTING a thick rhizome with a razor blade is risky. Handles for single-edge razor blades give you leverage and safety. The razor blade is inserted in a special holder at one end. Call your local hardware store to see if they stock this item, or can order. One alternative is a by-pass pruner, which must be sterilized before using on another plant.

them. If after a few minutes the plant is still not dislodged, run a sterile knife blade along the inside surface of the pot to loosen the roots, or cut or break the pot.

Step 2. Clean the plant of old potting mix and dead roots Some growers trim roots that are especially long, 6 inches or more, or those that are broken.

Step 3. Select a pot Choose a container that will accommodate at least two years' worth of growth. To do this, place the plant so that its oldest pseudobulbs (called backbulbs) are against the rim of the pot. Now examine how much space there is between the front growth(s) and the edge of the container. If that distance roughly equals the length between the first and third pseudobulb from the front, the pot size is correct. Add some drainage material if it is needed.

It is important not to overpot. Cattleyas do not like pots that are too big, so do not put your plant in a pot that could accommodate more than two new growths. The bigger the pot, the greater the chance of the medium taking too long to dry and the roots not getting enough air. This could lead to root rot, endangering your plant.

Orchids That Do Not Like Pots

NOT all orchids grow well in clay or plastic pots. Vandas and related genera (called vandaceous orchids) prefer to grow in slatted baskets. The space between the slats allows for ample air infiltration. Coarse potting media, such as chunks of charcoal (not briquettes) and tree fern, are used with these orchids to further increase air reaching the roots. Even so, in short order most vandaceous roots end up outside their basket, hanging freely in the air, the way they do in nature.

Above: Stanhopea graveolens 'Planting Fields', CBM/AOS.

Species of *Stanhopea* and *Dracula* are grown in baskets for another reason: their inflorescences grow straight down. Circular wire, wood-slat or plastic-mesh baskets hold the potting medium and roots, while allowing inflorescences to develop freely. If potted in a conventional pot, *Stanhopea* and *Dracula* inflorescences would never emerge to see the light of day.

Step 4. Consider dividing the plant Breaking the plant apart may be necessary if it will not fit in a pot any smaller than 8 to 10 inches in diameter. Often, removing one or two backbulbs will reduce the plant's bulk so it will slip into the container. Larger pots are cumbersome, and as just mentioned, risky to the plant's health. To divide a cattleya, select that point on the rhizome where, when divided, the resulting pieces will have at least four pseudobulbs apiece. Using a sterile cutting edge, make a clean cut. Now continue.

Step 5. Position the plant in the pot The backbulbs should be against one side, and the rhizome approximately 1 inch below the rim. Make sure there is enough room in front of the lead bulb (if not, use a larger pot, or further divide). Now fill in with the potting mix, packing firmly. Make sure the rhizome stays at or near the top of the medium.

Step 6. Stake if necessary This is especially true for tall or large cattleyas. If you are using a hanger to suspend the plant, attach it to the pot and secure one pseudobulb or more to the hanger itself with ties and without undue bending. If the plant is top-heavy and you do not have a hanger, use a dowel or other stake. Drive it into the center of the pot (avoiding the rhizome) and secure the nearest pseudobulbs to it with ties that will not cut the tissue.

Rhizome clips, available from garden centers or mail-order orchid suppliers, are excellent for securing cattleyas and other sympodial orchids. They are sturdy rods with a kink at one end. This end clips over the edge of the container, while the straight end is placed over the rhizome and holds it in place. Remove the clip once the orchid has established itself firmly in the container.

Step 7. Transfer the label Write the month and year on the back of it so you know when you last repotted. If you have made a division, make sure you make an additional label for it. An unidentified orchid is of little use to anyone.

Above: Ascocentrum aurantiacum is among those epiphytic orchids that do well when grown in a wooden slat basket with a few pieces of charcoal, or nothing at all, placed around the roots. Be sure to use charcoal for growing plants, not the kind for your barbeque.

Special Care for Your Repotted Orchid

No matter how carefully you repot your orchid, it is going to undergo a mild shock until new roots become established in the fresh potting medium. During this time, which may last up to a month or two:

- Reduce the amount of light the plant receives.
- Water less often, perhaps half the frequency you normally would. (Some growers recommend not watering at all, but misting occasionally. If you grow indoors where humidity levels are low this might be too dry.)

What do you do when something goes wrong with your orchid? The next chapter discusses some common problems that beginning orchid growers may encounter when cultivating their plants.

Mounted Orchids

SOME orchids are best grown the natural way: mounted on (what once was) another plant. Slabs of cork bark or tree fern are most commonly used for this purpose. Smaller orchids are more practical for mounting. Some species will not grow successfully any other way.

Attach the plant to the slab with monofilament fishing line. Held firmly in place, new roots quickly attach, rambling over and, in the case of tree fern, through the slab. When an orchid outgrows its slab, the smaller slab can be attached piggyback fashion onto a larger one.

Growing mounted orchids under conventional conditions indoors is a challenge. Low humidity levels stress most orchid roots so exposed to the air. But if you grow outdoors much of the year, you may want to make your next purchase a mounted orchid. There is something right and satisfying about growing orchids nature's way.

Below: Cord and u-hooks secure a *Trichocidium* Elvena to a piece of cork. Provide bright light and perfect drainage for success.

Above: Hanging orchids mounted on pieces of cork on wire fencing material enhances air circulation around the plants.

Above: Delightful fragrance is a trademark of *Brassavola nodosa.*
Below: A miniature worthy of cultivating on a mount is *Sophronitis acuensis* 'Bronstein-Walsh', AM/AOS. This specimen was grown on a piece of tree fern.

5 ~ What's Wrong With It?

Above: When cared for properly, many orchids, including *Dendrobium* Upin Red 'Mini' (Oberon x Super Star), reward growers with their remarkable flowers. Failure to bloom often signals something is wrong with the cultural practices. Talk with fellow members at your local orchid society or a commercial grower to help pinpoint the problem and develop a solution.

YOU HAVE HAD YOUR FIRST ORCHID for some time now, and yet it is not prospering. Few, if any, flowers have opened. Why? This chapter will outline common problems faced by beginning orchid growers, why they happen and what can be done to solve them.

Cultural Practices
More often than not, if your orchid is not growing well, it has something to do with how you are growing it, not with a pest

or disease. Such problems are due to your cultural practices.

Overwatering   After growing other plants in soil mixes, growing orchids in bark and other media for epiphytes is an adjustment — within hours of watering these media appear dry. Because of this, many beginners tend to overwater their first orchids.

Symptoms: Two things can happen when an orchid is overwatered:

- The medium does not have a chance to dry out. The pores, spaces in the medium normally filled with air, are filled with water. Without sufficient oxygen, the plant's roots are unable to function fully. If these conditions persist, the roots die.

  Unable to take up enough water because of this loss of roots, the plant gradually wilts. Pseudobulbs, once plump and smooth, now have deep furrows running lengthwise. Leathery leaves curl, soften and develop creases. Thinner leaves may never expand fully. Older leaves turn yellow and drop prematurely.

  Understandably, beginners can easily interpret this to mean their orchid needs more water, not less. They water more, and the plant gets sicker.
- The weakened plant develops black rot, *Pythium* or *Phytophthora*. In a matter of days, the plant turns black, usually from the bottom up, and dies.

What to do: Usually, by the time you realize you have been overwatering, your plant's roots, and the potting medium, are in a state of decay. Repot as soon as possible. Remove all decayed roots. Use a coarser grade of medium. Larger pieces of medium mean larger pores and more rapid drying. Being virtually rootless, the plant will probably need additional support. Use rhizome clips or support the plant with pot rings that clip onto the rim of the container.

From now on, water more carefully. Be sure that your orchid dries out sufficiently between waterings. Remember to water from above and let the water drain through the holes in the bottom of the container.

If your plant has no viable roots, after repotting and watering, place the plant and container in a clear plastic bag. Loosely tie the bag closed. This will prevent the orchid from drying out further by greatly reducing evaporation. Place the bagged plant in a location that receives indirect light only until you see evidence of new roots forming. Then remove from the bag and continue to grow the plant, watching closely to see if any other problems develop.

(Note: Be sure that while it is in its bag, a rootless orchid is not exposed to direct sunlight. Sunlight would lead to a build up of heat within the bag, "cooking" the plant in a matter of hours.)

If your orchid has developed black rot, treat it immediately with the appropriate fungicide. The identification and control of orchid diseases is discussed in Chapter 6.

Underwatering   A few beginning orchid growers have the reverse tendency: they underwater. They place their first orchid in a sunny window or outdoors, and forget about it until the weekend, when thoughts naturally turn to hobbies. Meanwhile, it is possible that the plant could have benefited from a midweek watering. Or, they take warnings about overwatering too much to heart, and merely sprinkle or mist their orchid rather than flushing it with water when it is dry.

Symptoms: Indications of underwatering are, ironically enough, the same as when an orchid is overwatered to the point of root loss. Either way, the plant is not getting enough water, and wilts. See the symptoms for overwatering listed above.

The thinner leaves of some orchids, such as miltonias, may exhibit accordion-like pleating as they develop. These leaves,

For indoor growers, low humidity is a common problem that can reduce the vigor of your plants. Means of increasing humidity include operating a humidifier, placing the plant on a tray of gravel filled with water and, where possible, growing outdoors.

Too Little Light   Energy is required for an orchid to grow and flower. Through photosynthesis, plants convert sunlight into a form of energy they can store and use. Without adequate light, a plant cannot accumulate enough energy reserves to support abundant growth and flowers. Orchids, like other flowering plants, need a minimum amount of light to prosper.

Symptoms: Your orchid is not receiving enough light if:

- It is dark green, but lusterless, while appearing to have an intact root system.
- Each new leaf or growth is smaller than the last.
- The plant looks floppy and weak overall.
- It has produced only a flower or two, if any.

What to do: Increase the amount of light your orchid receives, but be careful to do it gradually. Leaves become tender when they receive inadequate light and can easily burn (see below) if suddenly exposed to dramatically higher light conditions.

If you are growing under lights, move your plant closer to the tubes and toward the center of the fixture where light intensities are at their highest. If you are not already doing so, operate your lights at least 14 hours a day, preferably 16. If it has been more than one year since you have replaced the tubes, do so as soon as possible. Older tubes put out much less light.

Orchids grown on windowsills should be moved to another window, one with one or two hours more direct sunlight. Turn the plant frequently and check it every day for evidence of burning. If the plant begins to show signs of too much light, provide some

Above: This cymbidium's healthy root system is a sign of proper watering, where the medium is kept evenly moist and not too wet.

instead of expanding fully, emerge heavily creased horizontally, and stay that way.

What to do: First, make certain that your plant suffers from underwatering, not overwatering. Check the state of its root system: Is the plant secure in its container, or is it wobbly? If it is loose, repot. Follow the instructions above.

If your plant seems well-rooted, increase your watering frequency. If you have been watering once a week, water twice; if you have been watering twice a week, water every other day. When you do water, water thoroughly — until the water comes gushing out of the pot's bottom.

Watch the plant closely to see if it responds. Signs of wilting should lessen; leaves often take on a healthier, deeper shade of green. (Accordion leaves, however, will not right themselves. Watch newly emerging leaves for proper development.)

If, after increasing your watering frequency, your plant still appears wilted, insufficient humidity may be the culprit.

shading, either with a semitransparent curtain, other plants or cheesecloth. After a month, when the plant has adjusted to the new environment, reduce or remove the shading material.

Too Much Light   Damage, frequently referred to as "burning," can result from too much light.

Symptoms: Dry yellow patches on the leaves are the first indication that an orchid is getting too much light. On a thick-leaved orchid, such as a cattleya, these patches are often rough and slightly raised. If you suspect a plant is receiving excessive light, feel the leaf. Leaves at or near the point of burning feel hot to the touch. This is especially true of leathery leaves.

If conditions persist, the yellow patches will grow more numerous, darken to black, and sometimes become sunken (if the leaves are thick). Eventually the leaves will drop off. Under extreme conditions, an entire plant can be lost.

Orchids that have been under conditions that are too bright, but not excessively so, may become yellowish and stunted.

What to do: Reduce the amount of direct sunlight your plant is receiving. Either move the plant to a location that receives less sunlight each day, or provide shade. Burn patches will stop spreading, and the plant should become more green.

Prevention Tips

MAINTAINING a clean growing area is the first step toward preventing diseases from infecting an orchid collection, whether it is a few plants on a windowsill or hundreds in a greenhouse. Every time you water, remove any dead leaves or blossoms from the plants and take them out of the growing area. Proper spacing of plants and maintaining constant air circulation are important, too. During the winter it is especially important to watch your plants and take immediate action should a disease appear.

However, once tissue has been burned, the damage remains, so do not expect burned leaves to look unscathed again.

If you grow outdoors, you may find that too much light is a problem during certain seasons of the year and not others. Spring is a season to be especially wary of burning — your plant has become accustomed to the lower light and cooler conditions of winter. (If the plant has been inside all winter, this is especially true.) But now the sun is climbing in the sky and is more intense, and temperatures are rising. At the same time, deciduous plants have yet to put on their leaves and provide shade.

Remember, growing conditions are rarely static. Constantly observe your orchid and be ready to respond to any changes.

Low Temperatures   Freezing temperatures, below 32 F (0 C), cause ice crystals to form in susceptible plant tissue, lacerating it like countless tiny knives. Temperatures above freezing, but below optimum for a genus (see the Temperature and Orchids table on page 10), cause more subtle problems.

Symptoms: Within hours of exposure to freezing temperatures, orchid tissue turns dark and mushy. This can happen to a single leaf that is touching a windowpane on a frosty night, or to an entire plant left outdoors during freezing weather.

An orchid grown under temperature conditions below its optimum, but which are not freezing, becomes weakened over time. Weakened orchids are more susceptible to various fungi and bacteria, including those that cause leaf spotting and rot.

What to do: Lowest temperatures prevail during winter nights, so if you grow indoors, either move your orchid away from windows, where temperatures are the lowest, or turn up the thermostat. Sheets of bubblepack applied to windows help to insulate the growing area. If you grow outdoors, bring in your plant on those nights when temperatures of 50 F (10 C) are forecast for two hours or more.

Above: Excessive light causes leaves to burn, leaving ugly marks like the one on this *Cattleya* Irene Holguin (Astral Beauty x J. A. Carbone).

High Temperatures Orchids also have a limited tolerance of temperatures that are too high. Sustained temperatures above the optimal range can cause serious harm. A chart of acceptable temperatures is given on page 10.

Symptoms: Extremely high temperatures, in combination with intense light, cause the same yellowing and blackening of leaf tissue mentioned earlier under the heading, "Too Much Light." Temperatures consistently above an orchid's preference can result in leaf-tip die-back, a necrosis (death) of leaf tissue near the end of the leaf. Leaf drop, as well as malformed growths and leaves, are also indications of excessively high temperatures. Some particularly sensitive orchids, like masdevallias, will literally fall apart in hot weather.

Orchids that experience night temperatures significantly above recommended levels can become weakened by the resulting imbalance of respiration (which uses en-

ergy reserves) and photosynthesis (which makes them). High temperatures at night, when respiration is at its peak, can cause a plant to expend too much energy, resulting in weak, leggy growth.

What to do: Reducing the temperature is harder than increasing it, especially indoors. If you are not growing outdoors during the summer when high temperatures are a problem, consider moving your orchid outside. On all but the warmest nights, your orchid will experience a far more suitable drop in night temperature than indoors.

Other means of moderating temperature include:

- Increasing air movement. Keep the air circulating around a plant to increase transpiration (evaporation from the leaves), which has a cooling effect. Moving air also moderates temperature, removing pockets of hot air.
- Reducing the amount of light. Sunlight is a tremendous source of heat within a plant's tissue. Lowering the number of hours a plant receives sunlight, and breaking up the light reaching the plant through various means of shading, help reduce the plant temperature.
- Selecting genera suitable to prevailing conditions. If you are growing orchids under warmer temperatures, grow warm-growing orchids. Do not try to fight your conditions, or your orchid, and you, will suffer.

Too Little Fertilizer Orchids are rarely fast growers, so they do not require copious amounts of fertilizer. Symptoms of underfertilizing are rare, and hard to identify.

Symptoms: The most obvious symptom of consistent underfertilizing (virtually no fertilizer at all) would be smaller leaves and growths. The entire plant is apt to appear yellowish. This would be most apparent in orchids grown in inorganic media, which offer no nutrition to the plant.

Organic media release some nutrients as they decompose.

What to do: Apply a suitable fertilizer at the recommended frequency and rate (see pages 16 and 17 for information on this subject).

Too Much Fertilizer Overfertilizing is more common. It is tempting to use too much of a good thing.

Symptoms: With sustained overfertilizing, salts build up in the growing medium. A white crust forms around the inside rim of the pot and, in some cases, on top of the medium itself. When orchid roots come into contact with these salts, their growing tips turn black and die. If these conditions continue, whole roots can succumb. The plant will desiccate. Tips of leaves can also die due to over fertilizing.

What to do: Once symptoms such as these appear, the best thing to do is to repot. Be sure to cleanse the roots of any salt residues. Cut back your fertilizing to the recommended frequency and amount.

Recognizing ailments due to cultural practices is only part of the equation to raising healthy orchids. Often, a cure can be had by changing how you care for the plants. For example, if rot is a problem, providing less water and increasing air circulation may solve the problem. Consult with other orchid growers for advice.

Troubleshooting Guide for Beginning Orchid Growers

Symptom	What to do
Shriveled leaves/pseudobulbs	Check the plant's roots. If in good shape, increase watering. If in bad shape, repot and reduce watering frequency.
Rotting leaves/pseudobulbs	If cattleya, drench with Truban. Repeat in a few days. If phalaenopsis or paphiopedilum, spray with Physan. Repeat in a few days.
Dry, rough, yellow to brown or black patches on leaves	Too much light—shade your plant.
Smaller growths and leaves	Check condition of roots; repot if poor. If the roots are healthy and the leaves dark green, gradually increase light, watching for burning (above).
Leaves spotted or streaked in black	Caused by assorted fungi, or virus. Increase air movement around plant. Spray or dip with fungicide appropriate to disease and available in your state. If necrosis continues on new leaves, have tested for virus.
Flowers streaked in darker color or black	Could be genetic defect, or virus. Consider having tested.
Roots in poor shape, tips turning black	Repot. Follow recommended fertilizing practices. If condition persists, have water tested — could be high in salts.
Few or no flowers	Is the plant mature, or an unflowered seedling or mericlone? Check for evidence of previous flowering. If present, check roots. If unhealthy, repot. If healthy, gradually increase light. Fertilize as recommended.
General lack of vigor	Make sure temperature conditions are optimal for genus (with proper 15 F [10 C] drop at night), and potting medium in good condition. If plant fails to thrive, have tested for virus.

6 ~ Diseases and Insects

OPTIMUM GROWING CONDITIONS make for healthy orchids that are resistant to disease. But even healthy orchids suffer to some degree from the various common pathogens.

In the previous chapter, we examined some of the physiological problems that affect orchids. Here, diseases, viruses and insects are discussed.

Whatever solution is recommended, take precautions to safeguard your health and that of others around you, including pets: read the label thoroughly, follow directions, and have the telephone number of a local emergency room or poison-control center written down in a convenient location.

Diseases

Black Rot These fungi — *Pythium ultimum* and *Phytophthora cactorum* — can kill an orchid quickly, so keep an eye out for the following symptoms of infection.

Symptoms: Black rot is an apt name for these pathogens. Infected areas, which can be any part of the plant, turn black and watery. The leading edge of the infection can appear fluid — much like a fast-rising black tide. Cattleyas are most often attacked. If the infection starts in or reaches the rhizome and the plant is not treated, in a matter of days it will be dead.

What to do: If the infection is isolated in the pseudobulb or leaf, remove it. Spray or drench with an appropriate fungicide available in your state at label strength and recommended frequency. A change in cultural practices coupled with removal of infected tissue is the best solution. Watch the plant until you are sure the infection has stopped progressing.

Root Rot As the name implies, root rot, caused by the fungus *Rhizoctonia*, typically attacks the roots. Orchids in decayed potting media, or those that are poorly aerated, are most susceptible.

Symptoms: Root rot is not usually as swift a killer as black rot. Infected roots eventually die, and after some time the rhizome is affected. Infected tissue appears more brown than black. The most noticeable symptom is a decline in the vitality of the infected plant, including shriveled pseudobulbs and leaves, and smaller new growths.

What to do: Unpot the infected plant, remove all diseased tissue, repot in fresh potting medium and drench with a recommended fungicide, following the instructions on the label. Repeat the fungicide in a week.

Bacterial Brown Spot This disease is most prevalent in phalaenopsis, and is as deadly as black rot is with cattleyas. It is

especially active under wet and cool conditions.

Symptoms: Infection by *Pseudomonas cattleyae*, the bacterium involved, starts as a brown, watery blister on a leaf and quickly spreads, engulfing whole leaves. If it reaches the growing center (the crown), then the plant is essentially gone.

What to do: Act immediately. Remove infected leaves with a sterile cutting edge. Spray immediately with Physan at the rate of ¹/₂ tablespoon per gallon of water. Repeat in a few days.

Brown Rot   This rot, caused by the bacterium *Erwinia cypripedii*, plagues paphiopedilums in particular.

Symptoms: Infection starts as a small brown spot on a leaf, but spreads quickly,

Opposite: Mites are difficult to see, but the damage they do is easily detected. They suck dry the leaves they attack, causing infested leaves to look silvery and dry. Here, mite damage is evident on the leaf of an *Opsistylis.*
Above: Botrytis cinerea is a fungus that spots orchid flowers. It is a problem when humidity levels are so high as to lead to water condensation on the flowers. Black dots on the flower, here a cattleya, can coalesce in severe infections.

forming a chestnut-brown patch. Infected plants give off an unusual, almost spicy odor. If the infection reaches the base of a paphiopedilum, it can kill the entire plant.

What to do: Remove infected leaves. Treat immediately as above for *Pseudomonas*, bacterial brown rot. Repeat in a few days.

Leaf-spotting Fungi Many fungi infect orchid leaves, but unlike the pathogens above, they are not usually lethal. Most growers, and their orchids, just live with them.

Symptoms: The fungi involved, *Cercospora* species for the most part, cause varying degrees of brown to black spotting on the leaves (and sometimes the pseudobulbs).

What to do: Several fungicides are available that can be sprayed onto orchids regularly. Making sure the plant has adequate ventilation, and is being grown under optimum conditions, helps reduce leaf-spotting.

Petal Blight *Botrytis cinerea* is a fungus that spots orchid flowers. To infect, it requires water on the flower surface, so it is a problem when humidity levels are so high as to lead to water condensation on the flowers. Water persisting on flowers after a rain or watering will encourage *Botrytis*.

Organic Solutions

BEFORE reaching for an insecticide, consider using a natural control that will eliminate an insect without harming the environment. Sunspray Ultra Fine Spray Oil, Safer's Insecticidal Soap and Wilder's Hot Pepper Wax are among the organic sprays for insects that are relatively nontoxic. In addition, there are predatory insects that can be released into the growing area that will destroy undesirable insects that threaten your orchids. Before making a decision, consult with an experienced orchid grower or your County Cooperative Extension Agent.

Symptoms: Black dots appear on the flower and, in severe infections, can coalesce.

What to do: Although a fungicide can be applied, once a flower is spotted, the damage is done. Increasing the air movement and decreasing the humidity will help keep the flowers dry, thereby minimizing the chances of infection. When watering, keep water off of the flowers. Remove infected flowers from the growing area to reduce sources of reinfection.

Viruses

Viruses plague orchids as they do most living things. Two viruses are prevalent among orchids: cymbidium mosaic virus (CyMV) and tobacco mosaic virus (TMV).

Symptoms: Classic symptoms of CyMV include sunken spots and lines of necrotic (dead) tissue on leaves. Similar necrosis can also appear in the flowers. TMV causes similar symptoms, but can induce color break (streaks of darker coloration) in flowers. Contaminated plants do not necessarily have obvious symptoms, though most plants exhibit a lack of vigor.

What to do: You may not know whether any orchid you buy is virused, but the seller should. Inquire whether the grower takes control measures for virus, and tests regularly. Consider using one of the virus testing services available (see advertisements in *Orchids*) for your plant.

Most importantly, always use sterile cutting edges to avoid transmitting the virus from one plant to another. As mentioned in the first chapter of this book, single-edge razor blades are suitable for this purpose. If wiped clean and heated in an oven set at 300 F (132 C) or higher for one hour, they may be reused.

Viruses have been known to be transmitted by dirty pots. Clean all used pots thoroughly with a brush and then soak in a solution of household bleach (1 cup in a gallon of water) for 30 minutes to one hour. Allow to dry before reusing.

Viruses could also be transmitted by

dirty hands. Some growers use disposable plastic gloves when repotting more than one plant. They change gloves with each plant they repot. Remember, for many good reasons, including virus control, do not recycle used orchid-potting medium.

An additional precaution against transmitting viruses is to place a stack of unfolded newspapers on the potting surface, and remove one sheet each time you pot or repot a specimen.

All these practices are important because once a plant is infected with virus, it will stay that way — there is no practical cure.

Insects

Orchids in cultivation have their share of pests. Here are the most prevalent.

Scale   Quite a few species of scale infest orchids.

Symptoms: Scale usually appears as a circular raised mound attached to any part of the plant. Left to its devices, it can proliferate and take over a plant, killing tissue. Cattleyas are the most likely to be infested with scale.

Above: A variety of insects may chew orchid flowers and leaves. Here, a beetle wreaks havoc on a cattleya flower.

What to do: Beginners have the advantage of owning just a few plants. A cotton swab dipped in alcohol and applied to the scale can control minor infestations. Nontoxic oil sprays, or pesticides such as Malathion, offer stronger control. Be careful to follow directions and minimize your exposure, as well as that of others.

Mealybug   These insects are a particular problem with paphiopedilums and other leafy orchids.

Symptoms: The white, sticky infestations typically start as a patch under the leaves or in some other less than obvious location. Under warm conditions, they spread quickly. An infestation not controlled early can persist for years, weakening and even killing some plants.

What to do: The trick with this and all orchid pests is constant surveillance, so that you catch any infestation before the pest can multiply. An isolated mealybug can be killed with alcohol. An entrenched infestation requires repeated spraying with pesticides found at your garden center, such as Malathion.

Caution: Pesticides are potentially dangerous. Check the label for whether the chemical is recommended for orchids or ornamentals. Do not use it if it is not. Follow directions carefully. Wear a mask and gloves, and spray outside away from people and pets. Wash thoroughly after spraying, and store the pesticide in a cool, dry place out of the reach of children.

Mites These pests are hard to see — but the damage they do is not.

Symptoms: Mites suck dry the leaves they attack, so that infested leaves look silvery and dry.

What to do: Repeated spraying with an insecticidal soap offers some control. Commercial miticides offer more. Ask at your local orchid or garden center for recommendations.

Slugs Slugs are more a problem outdoors and in greenhouses than indoors.

These slimy mollusks have a cruel preference for orchid buds and flowers. A number of baits are available, though of limited effectiveness. Baits in pellet or meal form are scattered around the plants; liquid forms can be diluted and poured on the medium. Some growers spread diatomaceous earth for organic control. **Warning: Baits are toxic to pets.** Hobbyists over the years have placed shallow bowls of beer in the growing area with some success. Perhaps the best control is to check the plants at night with a flashlight, when slugs are most active, plucking and squashing any found.

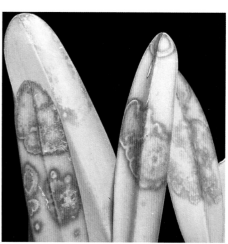

Right top: Slugs have a preference for orchid buds and flowers, although this one is consuming a phalaenopsis plant in a greenhouse.
Right middle: Bacterial rot manifests itself with watery brown spots and patches on leaves and pseudobulbs, including those of this *Miltassia* hybrid.
Right: Once infected with a virus, an orchid is impossible to cure. Tobacco mosaic virus, shown on this *Potinara* hybrid, induces sunken spots and lines of necrotic (dead) tissue on leaves.

Controlling Orchid Insects and Diseases

Pest or Disease	Symptoms	Treatment
Scale Genera most affected: *Cattleya* Alliance, though all susceptible	Circular white to off-white or brown bumps on any part of the plant	For small infestations, cotton swab dipped in alcohol; for more established infestations, spray with insecticidal soap; for severe infestations, spray with Volck Oil or other insecticide recommended for scale.
Mealybug Genera most affected: *Paphiopedilum*—though all orchids grown indoors are especially susceptible	Clumps of cottony plump insects	For small infestations, cotton swab dipped in alcohol; for more established infestations, spray with insecticidal soap; for severe infestations, spray with Malathion or other insecticide recommended for mealybug.
Mites Genera most affected: Those that have thinner leaves, such as *Cymbidium, Cycnoches*	Dry flecking of thin-leaved orchids, dusty in appearance, particularly on the underside of the leaves.	For minor infestations, spray repeatedly with insecticidal soap; for more serious attacks, spray with one of several available miticides.
Black rot, *Pythium* and *Phytophthora* Genera most affected: *Cattleya* Alliance	Black, mushy leaves and pseudobulbs	Drench with an available fungicide, following label directions. Repeat as needed.
Root rot, *Rhizoctonia* Genera most affected: *Cattleya* Alliance	Brown rot of roots and rhizomes, often starting in the middle of the plant	Drench with an available fungicide, following label directions. Repeat as needed.
Bacterial brown spot and brown rot, *Pseudomonas* and *Erwinia* Genera most affected: *Phalaenopsis, Paphiopedilum*	Watery brown spots and patches on leaves	Treat immediately with Physan, $1/2$ teaspoon per gallon. Repeat in a few days.
Leaf-spotting fungi, *Cercospora* and others All genera of orchids susceptible.	Various dark spotting on leaves	Increase air movement. Spray with a recommended fungicide according to label. Repeat periodically.
Petal blight, *Botrytis cinerea* Genera most affected: *Phalaenopsis, Cattleya*	Black dots on flowers	Increase air movement and lower humidity. Remove and dispose of infected flowers. Spray with a fungicide according to label directions. Repeat as needed.

An Ounce of Prevention

No pest, disease or cultural problem need kill your orchid — if you take action early. Keep an eye on your plant. Check it every day. In this way you can spot problems before they take their toll. The best growers are excellent observers of their plants. They not only see a potential problem, they act quickly before much damage is done. Check the troubleshooting guide on page 39.

By now, if you are like most beginners, you are more than ready to buy more orchids. Chapter 7 provides some ideas as to what to look for in your next orchid and where to find it. When you make a purchase and bring it home, however, remember to isolate the new plant from your other orchids to prevent any pathogens on the newcomer from infecting your collection. With a modicum of effort, your new orchids will reward you with plenty of color for years to come.

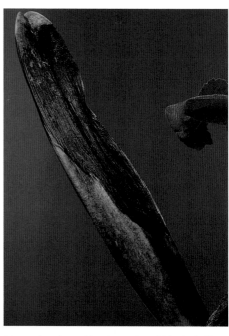

Above: A variety of fungi attack orchids, including this *Brassolaeliocattleya* hybrid.

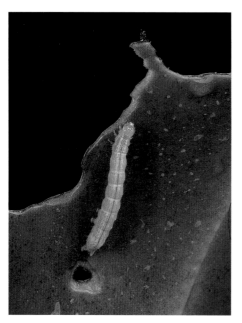

Above: A caterpillar eating a phalaenopsis leaf can cause damage that mars the leaf forever. By inspecting one's plants every day or two, many insect and disease problems can be prevented or at least eliminated in the early stages.

Above: Snails, which eat the roots and young shoots of orchids, may also consume mature leaves on phalaenopsis and other genera. Organic controls exist that will eliminate this pest without harming the environment.

Selecting Controls: A Shopper's List

SO that you can react quickly to a pest or disease attack on your orchids, keep certain basic supplies on hand. The following collection of less-toxic chemicals should control the most common offender.

Cotton swabs and rubbing alcohol Commonly available in grocery stores. Effective on the isolated mealybug or scale insect.

Spray bottle and measuring spoons While you have only an orchid or two, a simple plastic bottle with a fitted spray pump operated by hand should be adequate. Most garden centers sell spray bottles. For measuring the concentrate, be sure to buy a set of measuring spoons to be used for this purpose only.

Insecticidal soap Found in the organic section of your garden center, such soaps provide control of minor infestations of mealybug and scale. Must be used repeatedly.

Insecticide for control of scale and mealybug Entrenched infestations may require stronger sprays. Buy the smallest bottle of Volck oil, or any other insecticide whose label lists scale and mealybug control on ornamentals.

Fungicide for control of black rot Consult with a state agency for a recommended fungicide that can be applied to orchids. If one choice is unavailable, ask for another that controls "damping off" fungi (*Phythium* and *Phytophthora)* on ornamentals.

Bactericide to control bacterial brown spot and brown rot Physan is best for this. If your garden center does not carry it, ask for a bactericide that controls *Pseudomonas* and *Erwinia.*

Remember: Store all chemicals in a cool, dry place that is out of the reach of children. When administering, minimize your exposure to these chemicals by wearing plastic gloves and a mask, and spraying outside. Wash thoroughly afterward.

Above: Orchid literature is punctuated with the advice that air circulation will help prevent diseases from developing and harming plants. In an orchid nursery in Thailand, hanging vandas provides the air movement necessary for the plants to dry quickly after they are watered, thereby reducing the chance of infection by diseases. Placing the plants in wood slat baskets also helps keep fresh air around the roots and prevents water from accumulating.

7 ~ So You Want More

Above: Orchids are propagated several ways. Here are mericlones in flasks that should be genetically identical to the parent plant. Purchasing a mericlone assures that when the plant flowers, it will be the same size, shape and color as the flowers produced by the plant from which it was propagated.

Opposite: An inexpensive way to increase a collection is to purchase bare-root plants or divisions. When making a selection, choose divisions with healthy leaves and plump roots; avoid those with either mushy, wet roots or dry, papery roots, and shriveled pseudobulbs.

YOU HAVE MASTERED GROWING your first orchid, and now you want more. Before you buy your next one, consider the following.

How Was It Made?

How an orchid was propagated is important because it determines what you are getting. Orchids are commonly propagated one of three ways:

Division This is a form of asexual propagation; it does not involve a mixing of genes and thereby characteristics. When you get a division of a plant, the division's flowers will be the same as the original plant — and it will carry the same cultivar name (this is the name in single quotation marks following the specific epithet or hybrid name).

Mericloning This high-tech form of asexual propagation takes a single culti-

var and makes many copies of it. When you buy a mericlone, its flowers should be the same as any plant bearing the same (species/hybrid and cultivar) name. Unlike divisions, however, mericlones vary in maturity. Mericlone propagations fresh out of the bottle can be years from flowering. Divisions are typically within a year or two of flowering.

Seed This is sexual propagation, and results in a mixing of genetic characteristics, even if the orchid is self-pollinated. Flowers of seedlings run the gamut in appearance, often looking different from the parent(s). If you buy a seedling, expect the unexpected. This can be part of the fun.

Sources for Orchids

Four sources of orchids are available to most orchid growers:

Orchid Society Shows Most local orchid societies put on a show each year, often at a nearby mall. Shows are a great place to buy orchids. Any commercial growers in your area are likely to be there, as well as a few out-of-state firms. Call your local orchid society for the dates of the next show. American Orchid Society (AOS) Affiliated Societies and their representatives are listed by state or country in the *AOS Orchid Source Directory* sent to all new members of the AOS.

Orchid Society Auctions Most orchid societies conduct an annual auction to raise funds. At these auctions, members donate plants. Bidding for popular plants can be intense, but most orchids sold at auction go for bargain prices. Do not hesitate to ask the person next to you, or the auctioneer, if the plant "on the block" is suitable for beginners. Your local orchid society representative should know the date of the next auction. **Local Commercial Growers** Shows and auctions happen only once or twice a year. If you want to buy now, check the *AOS Orchid Source Directory* for the growers nearest you. Regular hours are listed. Still, it is best to call ahead before you visit. A description of the firm's general location is in the directory.

Mail Order Americans increasingly shop by mail, and orchids are no excep-

tion. Within the pages of orchid periodicals are pages of advertisements. Order away; it is a convenient way to shop.

Mail-order orchids are sold by two forms of measurement:

• Pot diameter (in inches). Cattleyas and other sympodial orchids are sold this way. Cattleyas listed with a pot size of 5 inches or more are generally considered flowering size.

• Leafspan (in inches). Phalaenopsis are usually sold this way. Leafspan is

---

What to Grow Where You Live

Where*	What
Temperate (New England, the Midwest and Pacific Northwest, Canada)	Cattleyas; cymbidiums; dendrobiums; masdevallias; miltonias; oncidiums; odontoglossums; paphiopedilums; phalaenopsis; and other intermediate- to cool-growing species and hybrids
Subtropical (South Florida)	Cattleyas; dendrobiums; warmer-growing miltonias, oncidiums, and paphiopedilums; phalaenopsis; vandas; and other intermediate- to warm-growing species and hybrids
Tropical (Hawaii)	Cattleyas; dendrobiums; warmer-growing miltonias, oncidiums, and paphiopedilums; phalaenopsis; vandas; and other intermediate- to warm-growing species and hybrids
Arctic/Subarctic (Alaska, Canada)	Cattleyas; cymbidiums; dendrobiums; cooler-growing miltonias; oncidiums, odontoglossums, and paphiopedilums; masdevallias; and other cool-growing species and hybrids
Arid (Southwest, Texas, Interior California)	Cattleyas; dendrobiums; warmer-growing miltonias, oncidiums, and paphiopedilums; phalaenopsis; vandas; and other intermediate- to warm-growing species and hybrids
Mediterranean/Maritime (West Coast)	Cattleyas; cymbidiums; dendrobiums; masdevallias; miltonias; oncidiums; odontoglossums; paphiopedilums; phalaenopsis; and other intermediate- to cool-growing species and hybrids

* For when to grow outdoors or indoors, see the information sidebar "Where to Grow Based on Where You Live" on page 13.

---

measured from tip to tip of the uppermost leaves. Phalaenopsis listed with a leaf span of 6 to 8 inches or more are generally considered flowering size.

Try, at least at first, to buy flowering-size plants. You will see flowers sooner rather than later, and the larger the plant, the more resilient it is likely to be. Avoid ordering during the hottest or coldest times of the year. Plants can cook or freeze in transit. Growers often will not ship under adverse conditions.

Most orchids are shipped out-of-pot, bare-root, unless you specify in-pot (which usually costs more). When you receive your mail-order orchid, take it out of the

Recommended Orchids

Orchid	Desirable Traits	Suitable Regions
Ascocentrum miniatum and *Asctm. curvifolium* and their hybrids (ascocentrums and ascocendas)	Compact plants with brightly colored flowers, flowering more than once a year	Best in subtropical or tropical regions (Florida, Hawaii), but will grow in all but the coldest regions
Cattleya Alliance	Adaptable, easy to flower, showy; many awarded mericlones available	All regions
Cattleytonia Why Not	Compact, adaptable, frequent flowering; awarded mericlones available	Best in subtropical or tropical regions (Florida, Hawaii), but will grow in all but the coldest regions
Cymbidiums	Long-lasting waxy flowers on thick spikes; easy to grow if you have the room.	Best in regions without sustained heat; will only flower with cool summer nights
Dendrobium phalaenopsis hybrids	Long-lasting flowers on long spikes, plants in flower many months of the year; mericlones available	Best in subtropical or tropical regions (Florida, Hawaii), but will grow in all but the coldest regions
Paphiopedilum Maudiae and *Paph. concolor* (mottled-leaved paphiopedilums)	Attractive mottled foliage on compact plant; long-lasting flowers	All regions; during hot weather protect from sun and keep well watered
Phalaenopsis (white or pink) species and hybrids	Large, long-lasting flowers on long spikes in spring; very showy; medium-sized plants	Best in subtropical or tropical regions (Florida, Hawaii), but will grow in all but the coldest regions
Phalaenopsis (yellow to red) species and hybrids	Smaller, more star-shaped, waxy flowers on shorter spikes appearing more toward summer	Best in subtropical or tropical regions (Florida, Hawaii), but will grow in all but the coldest regions
Sophrolaeliocattleya Jewel Box 'Scheherazade', AM/AOS 'Dark Waters', AM/AOS	Abundant bright red flowers on medium-sized plants; mericlones available	All regions

box, remove all packing materials from around the plant and pot it immediately.

Treat as you would any newly repotted orchid, only realize that it has the added handicap of being unaccustomed to your conditions. Keep the plant under protected conditions until it adjusts and shows signs of growth. For that matter, treat any orchid you receive, whatever its source, in this manner. Some growers isolate newly acquired plants until they are sure the plants harbor no pests or diseases.

The disadvantage of mail order, of course, is that you cannnot pick out the best plant. But most commercial growers go out of their way to sell quality plants. And if you are not happy with what they sent you — tell them. Reputable growers want to know if their customers are not satisfied, and will make amends.

What to Look For
in Your Next Orchid

Just glance at any orchid periodical, including *Orchids*, and you can see there are hundreds of different orchids from which to choose. Before you buy that next orchid, ask yourself:

• Is it suitable for my area? Each region has its own set of environmental conditions. Even if you grow indoors, your orchids are affected by what goes on outside. Give yourself and your orchid a fighting chance to succeed; choose what will grow well in your area.

Nearly all orchid societies have plant tables at their meetings where members show off their flowering orchids. It is like a mini-show each month. These plant tables will give you a good idea of what grows well in your area. A list of recommendations is provided on page 50.

• Is it suitable for my growing conditions? Just because some local hobbyists can grow a particular orchid well does not mean you will have the same success. Growers with greenhouses are likely to be able to grow orchids you may find a struggle. Consider your individual grow-

ing equation. For example, it might be best, at least at first, to stay away from any hybrids or species (such as *Masdevallia*) requiring cooler temperatures, constant humidity, and ample air movement.

If the answer to either question above is no for a particular orchid, think twice before buying it. If you are not so sure, ask the seller questions about its cultural needs.

Desirable Traits in Orchids

All orchids are not alike. All growers are not alike. Many beginners, though, prefer maximum show for minimum effort. The following list of orchids recommended for beginners is based on these criteria:

• Compactness. Orchids are like cars. In the '50s and '60s, with cheap energy, no one cared much whether an orchid was big or small. It was economical to heat a greenhouse whose spacious interior could hold an assortment of large orchids. Today, you can still find oversized plants, but there are a lot more miniature species and hybrids available. Many miniatures are nearly as showy as the orchids of the past — they are just a fraction of the size.

• Adaptability. Some orchids are highly particular about growing conditions. Others adjust well to a range of conditions. Adaptable orchids offer a better chance of success for any grower.

• Long-lasting flowers. Flower longevity in orchids varies tremendously, from less than one week to months.

• Frequent flowering. On the other hand, a plant that flowers three times a year, even if the flowers only last a week each time, might be a good choice.

• Presentation. Some orchids present their flowers proudly on upright spikes for all to see. Others hide them behind their leaves. Both are of interest, but initially you probably want to go for show.

• Availability. Even if an orchid possesses all the above traits, it is of no use to you unless you can get it.

Orchids for Beginners

A list of orchids suitable for beginners is listed on page 51. What follows is a few general comments given alphabetically by genus or alliance (a group of related genera).

Ascocendas Thirty years ago, you rarely saw a flowering vanda that was not 4 or more feet tall. Today, thanks to hybridizing with *Ascocentrum,* a genus of miniature, brightly colored species, we have *Ascocenda* (*Vanda* x *Ascocentrum*) hybrids. These are generally smaller but flower just as frequently (three times a year or more) and last just as long (often a month or longer).

Cattleya Hybrids These orchids well deserve their popularity. Typically these are tough plants with a determination to flower. Today, more than in the past, a buyer has a choice between large plants with huge flowers, or smaller plants (called "mini-catts") with smaller flowers — as well as everything in between. Many mericlones of awarded cultivars, some of which flower more than once a year, are available.

Top: Providing warm temperatures will coax this hybrid — *Vanda sanderiana* x *Ascocenda* Mildred Furumizo — to flower.
Above: Ascocenda Su-Fun Beauty 'Orange Belle' illustrates yet another color option in this genus of floriferous orchids.

Your First Orchid

Cymbidiums These orchids tend to be large plants requiring big pots, but if you have the room, and intermediate- to cool-growing conditions, try one. The long-lasting flowers are dramatic. Smaller hybrids and species are now available. Ask for them.

Dendrobium Phalaenopsis Hybrids These orchids are narrow but tall, although new hybrids are more compact than early introductions. Their pseudobulbs, which are skinny and long, are called "canes." *Dendrobium phalaenopsis* hybrids produce long spikes of flowers, usually more than one a year, often from the same pseudobulb. So if you have height in your growing area, and intermediate- to warm-growing conditions, consider trying one of the many *Dendrobium phalaenopsis* mericlones on the market.

Above: Cymbidiums are popular for their sprays of long-lasting flowers and can even be grown outdoors in Southern California and in other mild areas. *Cymbidium* Valerie Absolonova 'Talisman Cove', a compact hybrid with fragrant flowers, is suitable for intermediate temperatures.

Top: Many growers tout phalaenopsis as the ideal beginner's orchid. Among the many choices is this hybrid, *Phalaenopsis* Cloud of Butterflies. *Above:* Long-lasting medium-sized flowers are borne on this compact *Epicattleya* hybrid (*Cattleya forbesii* x *Epidendrum phoeniceum*).

Your First Orchid

Top: When shopping for ascocendas, be aware that many modern hybrids bloom two or three times annually. Among the numerous choices is *Ascocenda* Maui Beauty 'Ekahi', CR/HOS. *Above:* Masdevallias are small-growing orchids that put on a big show, making them ideal for growers with limited space. *Masdevallia* Confetti is at home in a plastic pot that helps keep the roots moist. Most masdevallias prefer cool temperatures, which is why they are not recommended for warm regions like Florida and Southern California.

Your First Orchid

Top: Phalaenopsis Violet King 'Talisman Cove' is another color variation among the moth orchids that are always popular with beginning hobbyists. Above: Dendrobium Sonia is one of many Dendrobium phalaenopsis hybrids that brighten the autumn with colorful flowers.

Opposite: Commonly called slipper orchids, the fascinating flowers of Paphiopedilum are long-lasting. Pictured here (clockwise from top) are Paphiopedilum Sibyl, Paphiopedilum Maudiae, Paphiopedilum Barbi Girl and Paphiopedilum Red Magic.

Your First Orchid

Top left: When shopping for orchids, ask dealers how large the plants will grow. Here, *Cattleya* Wavriniana towers above a compact *Epilaeliocattleya* Tinker Toy 'Sprite'.
Top right: Sophrolaeliocattleya Petite's Wink is small enough to grow on the windowsill.

Above: Brassolaeliocattleya Frank Fordyce 'Borneo Gal' can be placed in the art-shade category when describing color.
Opposite: Copious amounts of water are beneficial to *Zygopetalum* B. G. White 'Stonehurst' when potted in a porous mix.

Your First Orchid

Paphiopedilums There are orchidists who never think of growing any other genus than *Paphiopedilum* — and they never do. Paphiopedilums are more leafy and attractive than most orchids, and more compact. The flowers can last months. Be careful in your selection, though. There are paphiopedilums requiring cool growing conditions (generally they are the ones with solid green leaves) and paphiopedilums that tolerate warmer conditions (usually with mottled or patterned leaves).

Phalaenopsis These compact, monopodial orchids have rivaled cattleyas in popularity for years now, and with good reason. For show and ease of culture, they are tops. After decades of intense hybridizing, phalaenopsis flowers today come in a wide range of colors, sizes and shapes. Most plants stay in flower a month or two. The one drawback is that phalaenopsis are warmer growing and may suffer under constantly cool conditions.

Once you learn how to grow your first orchid, you will want to grow more. Developing friendships with fellow orchidists and joining an AOS Affiliated Society enhances this hobby.

Questions to Ask an Orchid Seller

AN orchid catches your attention, but you know nothing about it. Before you buy, wait until the seller has a free moment and then ask a few questions.

• "I grow [under lights, in a window, outdoors] in [location]. Will this orchid flower reliably under my conditions?"
• "How long until I can expect flowers?" (Ask this if the orchid is an unflowered seedling or mericlone.)
• "How often will it flower? How long do the flowers last?"
• "Does the plant have any special requirements I should know about?"

Once you have this information, you will be better able to make a wise decision whether or not to buy.

Opposite: Once you master the art of growing your first orchids, you'll possess the skills necessary to try more-challenging species, often called "botanicals." Among these are the two small-growing epiphytes shown here — *Psygmorchis pusillus* (in hand) best grown under intermediate conditions and *Ornithocephalus inflexus* (hanging) that requires humid shady conditions. Both can be attached to chunks of tree-fern fiber.

A Beginner's Orchid Library

PLENTY of information is available to help you grow better orchids, including the books listed here. All of these can be purchased through The AOS BookShop, which maintains a secured on-line ordering service at www.orchidweb.org. A booklist containing more than 250 orchid-related titles is published by the American Orchid Society once a year and mailed to members with their copies of *Orchids* magazine. A copy can also be requested from The AOS BookShop, 16700 AOS Lane, Delray Beach, Florida 33446-4351 (call toll free 1-877-ORCHIDS [672-4437] or dial 561-404-2020; fax 561-404-2100; e-mail TheAOS@aos.org).

American Orchid Society Guide Series
Growing Orchids, edited by James Watson. 2001 Revised Edition. Experts explain how to grow orchids and offer recommendations from *Anguloa to Zygopetalum.* More than 120 color photographs. Softcover. 108 pages.
Growing Orchids Under Lights, by Charles Marden Fitch. 2001 Revised Edition. A primer for growing orchids under fluorescent lights, plant lights and high-intensity lamps. 95 color photographs. Softcover. 76 pages.
Orchid Pests and Diseases. 2001 Revised Edition. Identification of ailments and their cures. More than 100 color and black-and-white photographs. Softcover. 118 pages.

Other References
Home Orchid Growing, by Rebecca Northen. 4th edition, 1990. The most popular orchid book for novice and experienced growers. 114 color photographs plus numerous black-and-white photographs. Hardcover. 384 pages.
Taylor's Guide to Orchids, by judywhite. 1996. A discussion on culture is complemented with a fully illustrated encyclopedia of types to grow. 302 color photographs. Hardcover. 385 pages.

Dear Gwen,
    Thank you for
the surprise visit-
It was a wonderful
Mother's Day - You
are such a joy! I
am so proud of
you and love
you very much.
        XXXOOX
            Mom

Index

Entries indexed include major subject headings and binomials in *italics*. Page numbers in **boldface** indicate illustrations.

International Orchid Center

THE American Orchid Society's International Orchid Center is a popular destination for anyone wishing to see live, flowering orchids and learn more about this dynamic family of flowering plants.

Conveniently located between Interstate 95 and the Florida Turnpike in Delray Beach, Florida, it offers:

• Educational presentations and programs.

• More than three-and-a-half acres of beautiful theme gardens, including a rainforest, Florida native habitat, formal garden, and the Lewis and Varina Vaughn Garden, which was built in loving memory of the Society's greatest benefactors.

• An orchid-filled greenhouse where visitors may stroll and enjoy the flowers.

• Seasonal displays of flowering orchids in a specially designed trellis.

• The Orchid Emporium, a tantalizing gift shop offering books, clothing, accessories and more.

Future additions for the orchid campus include a two-story library and an 80-seat auditorium for ongoing orchid education. AOS members are admitted to the International Orchid Center free of charge. Please come by for a visit — and then come again to enjoy new flowering orchids and witness botanical wonders as they unfold in our subtropical garden.

INTERNATIONAL ORCHID CENTER
16700 AOS Lane, Delray Beach, Florida 33446-4351
Tel 561-404-2000 • Fax 561-404-2100
E-mail TheAOS@aos.org • Web site orchidweb.org
The AOS BookShop and Orchid Emporium
Toll free 1-877-ORCHIDS or 561-404-2020